The Passover S[tory]
Told By Moses

We're working on an app! Join us now & get it for free when we launch.

Unlimited illustrated children's stories like this one that teach **your** values (history, religion, family, courage, kindness, and much more) in one app including animations, music, read aloud, and even an option to insert familiar family faces into the story!

We've all heard of Passover, but do you know the original story?
Fortunately for you, I was there!

My name is Moses, and this is why we still celebrate Passover to this day...

Over 3,000 years ago, a group of Jewish people called the Israelites arrived in Egypt for the very first time.

They were welcomed into Egypt thanks to a man called Joseph, who was second in command to the Pharaoh.
As long as Joseph was around, the Israelites were safe.

Over the years, the Israelites grew in numbers, and they became a big part of the community in Egypt.

Until one day, disaster struck. News travelled far and wide that Joseph had passed away!

A new Pharaoh rose to power and without Joseph by his side, he ruled with cruelty. The new Pharaoh decided that the Israelites were too powerful, so he came up with a plan. He put every last one of them into slavery!

The Israelites were forced to work in the boiling sun to build cities for the new Pharaoh. But still, they grew in number.

The Pharaoh was still scared of how powerful the Israelites were, so he ordered for all newborn Jewish boys to be killed

Meanwhile, across Egypt, a woman by the name of Jocheved gave birth to a baby Jewish boy. At first, she was able to hide the child, but soon it became impossible.

Jocheved decided that there was only one thing to do. She placed her baby boy into a basket and sent him floating down the River Nile. The baby's older sister, Miriam, watched the basket from the bushes to make sure he stayed safe.

A little way down the river, the Pharaoh's daughter was enjoying a bath in the water when she noticed the basket. She found the baby inside and quickly realised it was a Jewish boy, but decided to take him home anyway.

And do you know what she named the baby?

Moses! That's right! I'm the baby! What a twist!

Miriam ran after the Pharaoh's daughter and offered to find a wet-nurse for baby Moses. And who did she find to be the wet-nurse? Jocheved, of course! Baby Moses' actual mother!

The Pharaoh's daughter raised baby Moses like a son and he turned into a fine young man, if I do say so myself.

Years later, I was now a young man. I left the palace to explore Egypt and I didn't like what I found. I stumbled across an Egyptian man hurting a Hebrew man and I killed the Egyptian!

I was forced to flee Egypt to live in Midian as a shepherd.

One day, while looking after my sheep, I came across a burning bush. That's right! A bush... but on fire!

It turned out, the bush was actually a message from God! He told me to order the Pharaoh to let the Israelites go.

But no matter how many times I asked, the Pharaoh refused to follow God's orders.

He actually worked the Israelite slaves even harder!

"Why are you allowing this?" I asked God.
And he told me that a punishment was coming.

I went to see the Pharaoh again and again and again over the following days, but he refused to let the Israelites go. I tried to warn him about God's punishment, but he ignored me.

That's when the plagues came.
The Ten Plagues of Egypt!

First, God turned the Nile from water into blood.

Second, God sent a swarm of frogs to invade Egypt.

Third, God sent lice to infect all the men and animals.

Even after the third plague, the Pharaoh still refused to let the Israelite slaves go.

The fourth plague followed soon after, as hundreds of wild animals stormed into the city.

Fifth, all the animals in Egypt died. All the chickens, all the cows, all the horses, and all the dogs.

Sixth, the people of Egypt all grew nasty, painful boils on their bodies. Ouch!

Seventh, thunder and hail and fire rained down from the sky.

Finally, the Pharaoh agreed to let the Israelite men go... but he wanted to keep all of the women and children!

I refused. God wanted all of the Israelites to leave Egypt safely. Not just the men!

The Pharaoh said no, and so the eighth plague arrived.

This time, a swarm of locusts invaded Egypt and ate all the crops.

The ninth plague saw a thick darkness sweep over Egypt, removing all the light from the land.

But still, the Pharaoh refused!

So, God told the Israelites to all sacrifice a lamb and sprinkle its blood on their doorposts. If a door had lamb blood on it, the house would be spared from the tenth and final plague.

And so, at the stroke of midnight, on the 15th of the month of Nissan, the tenth plague arrived.

The first-born child of every Egyptian house was killed.

Finally, the Pharaoh gave up and followed God's orders.

He begged the Israelites to leave his land.

The Israelites left in such a hurry that their bread did not have time to rise.

On their way out of Egypt, they asked their neighbours for gold, silver and garments, leaving with many riches.

But the story does not end there!

Soon after the Israelites had set off, the Pharaoh decided to chase them and force them to return. We found ourselves trapped between the Pharaoh's army and the sea!

That's when God sent me one more message...

He told me to raise my staff over the water and when I did, something magical happened.

The sea split in half and allowed the Israelites to walk across the dry land in between!

When the Pharaoh and his army tried to follow,
the water closed once more and swept them away.

And that is why we celebrate the anniversary of Passover every year. And we still eat Matzah, the flatbread, to this day.

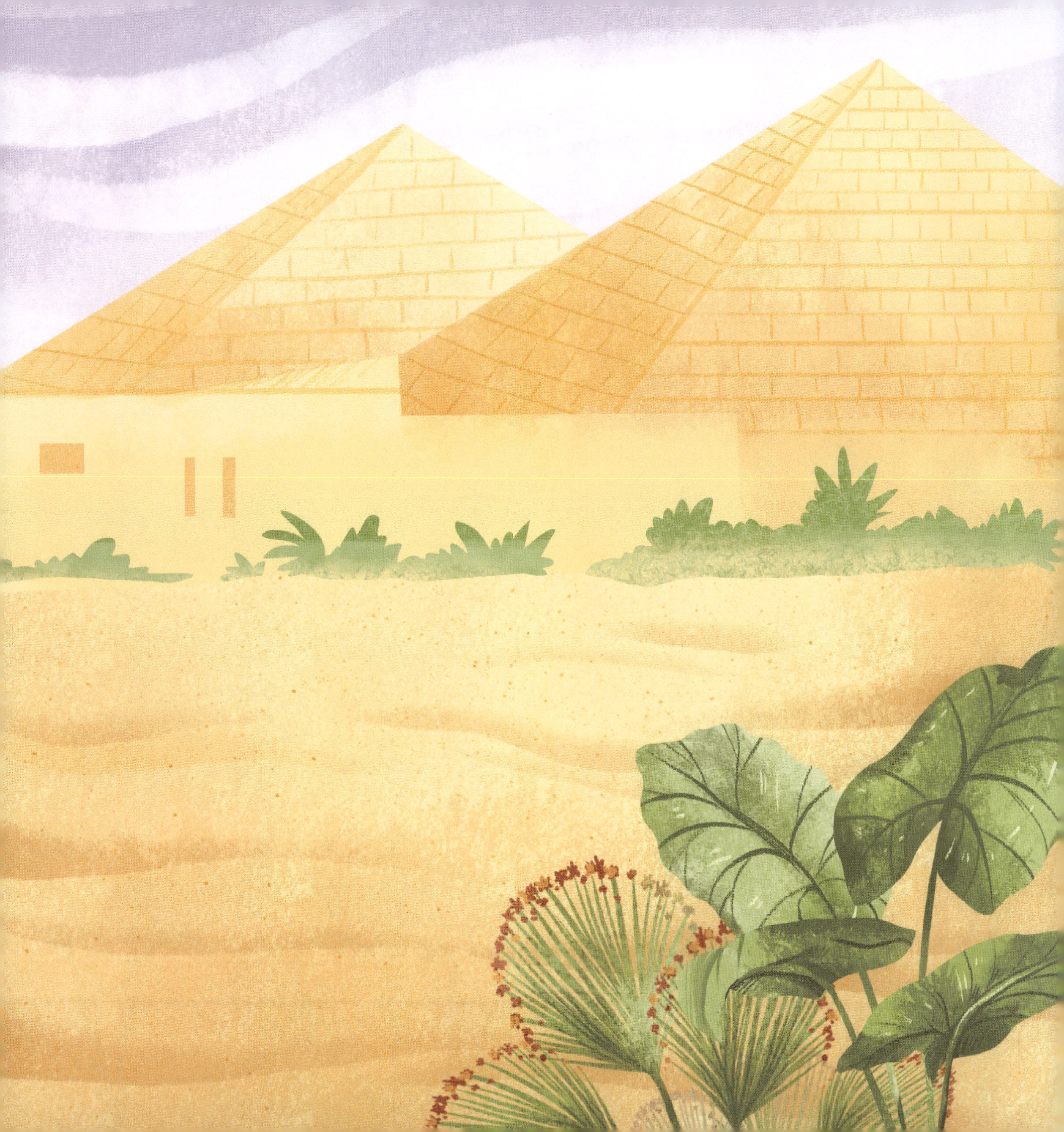

Printed in Great Britain
by Amazon